The Scottish-Island Girl

Joanne Gail Johnson

© Copyright text Joanne Gail Johnson 2001
© Copyright illustrations Macmillan Education Ltd 2001

All rights reserved. No reproduction, copy or transmission of this publication may be made without written permission.

No paragraph of this publication may be reproduced, copied or transmitted save with written permission or in accordance with the provisions of the Copyright, Designs and Patents Act 1988, or under the terms of any licence permitting limited copying issued by the Copyright Licensing Agency, 90 Tottenham Court Road, London W1P 9HE.

Any person who does any unauthorised act in relation to this publication may be liable to criminal prosecution and civil claims for damages.

First published in 2001 by
MACMILLAN EDUCATION LTD
London and Oxford
Companies and representatives throughout the world

www.macmillan-caribbean.com

ISBN 978-0-333-92091-6

10 9 8 7 6 5 4 3 2
10 09 08

This book is printed on paper suitable for recycling and made from fully managed and sustained forest sources.

Printed in Malaysia

A catalogue record for this book is available from the British Library.

Illustrations by VANESSA SOODEEN

'Are we nearly there yet?' asked Lizzy.

'Not yet, Lizzy,' said her mother. 'We're about half way there. I promise, it will be worth it.'

'This is a special adventure for your birthday!' said Alex. 'Thank you for inviting me, Mrs Steele.' Alex liked her new friend, and she liked her new friend's mother.

'Where were you born, Lizzy?' asked Alex.

'Scotland,' said Lizzy.

'And I was born here in Trinidad, like you, Alex,' said Lizzy's mother. 'We've lived in lots of countries. Scotland, America, Venezuela. But now I want Lizzy to see Trinidad, because I grew up here.'

'Do you like Trinidad, Lizzy?' asked Alex.

'Well, it's very different from Scotland,' said Lizzy. 'There are some things I don't like. The roads have huge potholes and there's messy bush everywhere. In some places there are no dustbins and people throw garbage everywhere … and it's too-oo-oo hot!'

'Well, of course it's hot,' said Alex. 'You're in the tropical rain forest, Lizzy.'

'It's not raining now,' said Lizzy.

'Well, no, it doesn't rain all the time,' said Alex. 'But there is a lot of rain that makes all kinds of plants grow really well – and great tall trees. And there are hundreds of different kinds of animals and birds and butterflies.'

'Wow!' marvelled Lizzy. She looked out of the window with more interest now.

Lizzy wanted to show off Scotland too, so she added, 'In Scotland we have a big, big, big monster called Nessie. It's a sort of dinosaur and it lives in a loch. Do you know what that is?'

'Something to keep the door shut?'

'No, silly, it's a lake!' Lizzy laughed. 'You spell it "l-o-c-h", not "l-o-c-k".'

'Well, monsters aren't for real, anyway. They're just made up. The things I'm telling you are fact,' Alex bounced back.

'I like Scottish dancing,' said Lizzy. 'The men wear kilts and the women have dresses with tartan sashes.'

'I like steel bands,' said Alex. 'When they play you just have to dance.'

'Look at that butterfly!' said Lizzy. 'It's huge! And what colours!'

'Let's count them,' said Alex.

'You count red ones and I'll count the others,' said Lizzy.

Mrs Steele smiled. The adventure was off to a good start.

At Grande Riviere they took their bags into the little guest house on the beach. The girls changed into their swimsuits. Alex ran down to the water and splashed in.

'It's wonderful!' she called.

'Ouch! Ow! Oh!' Lizzy complained. 'It's so stony! Come and give me a piggy back in, Mo-o-o-mmmmmy!'

'Come on, Lizzy!' Alex waved.

Lizzy wanted to hurry. 'But the stones hurt my feet!'

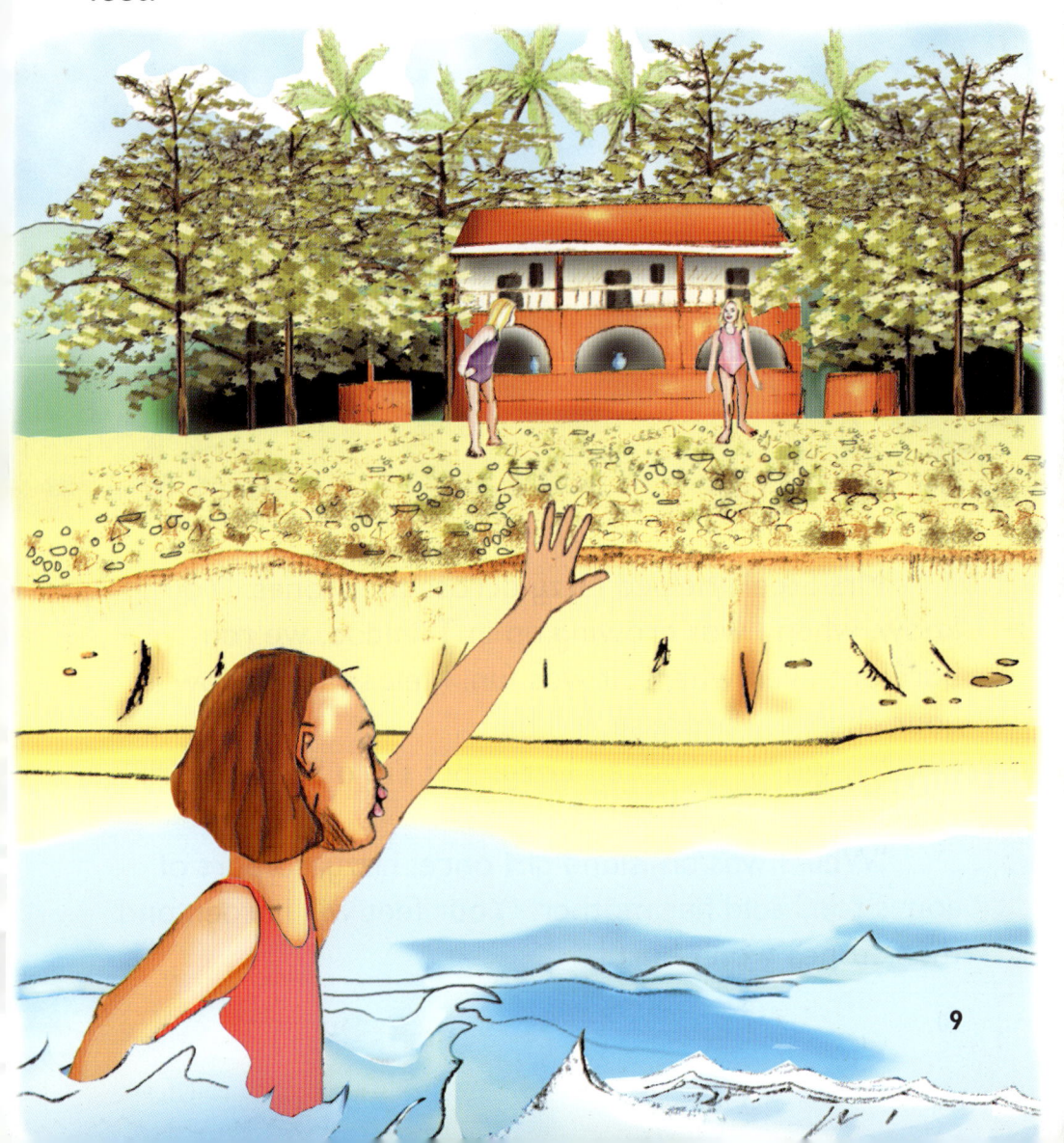

Mrs Steele helped Lizzy across the stones. 'You know, when I was growing up in Trinidad, we ran barefoot everywhere. It was fun. I felt so free. Now is your chance! I promise, it'll be …'

'… worth it.' added Lizzy. 'But I'm a Scottish girl, Mom, not an island girl like Alex.'

'Well, I was an island girl once, Lizzy, so part of you is too,' said her mother. 'Your feet will harden and then stones won't hurt.'

The water came up around Lizzy's ankles. It felt cool and playful. She felt sand between her toes again and plunged in.

Lizzy was a good swimmer, but a pool was not like the big waves of Trinidad's north coast. She watched as Alex rode over the smooth peaks, then she tried too.

'Hold your breath and go under when the waves come down to you,' said Alex.

Lizzy looked to the shore. Her mother was watching them. She felt safe.

'Rule number one, my grandpa taught me: Never turn your back to the sea' said Alex. 'Always keep an eye outward. Then you can see the waves coming.'

After lunch, Lizzy's mother took the friends to a river that came across the beach to the sea. 'So this is Grande Riviere, the big river,' said Lizzy.

They spent the afternoon skimming stones across it.

Lizzy scooped up some river water. 'How strange!' she cried. 'I can taste fresh river water and salty sea water. They're all mixed up.'

Then Alex noticed something and ran off. Lizzy dropped her stash of pebbles and followed.

'Almonds, Lizzy,' said Alex. 'Look at the tree. The leaves are so broad and the branches sprawl out just like this.'

The two girls giggled as they spread their arms and legs wide like the tree.

Alex took an almond and pounded it against a river rock. Inside was a small nut. She popped one in her mouth and dared her friend, 'Mmm. Try one, Lizzy!'

Lizzy copied her. 'Mmm, it's just like ones we buy at the store … but better! Let's take some to Mom.'

Lizzy's mother smiled when they gave her a handful of almonds.

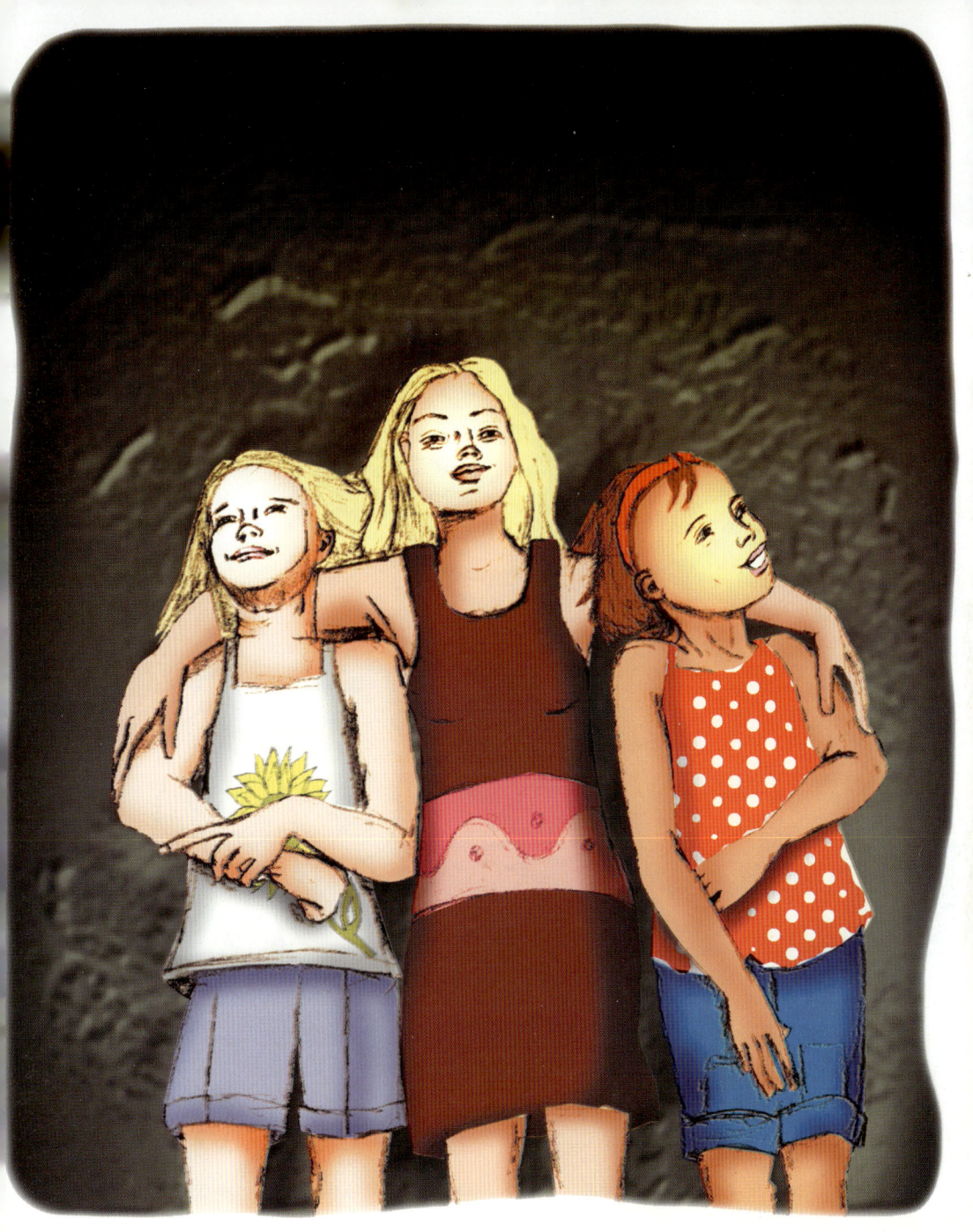

As darkness fell, all three lay out on the sand after dinner and looked at the stars in the sky. 'Two hundred and twenty-three … aw, Mrs Steele, we'll never be able to count them all. There are a gazillion stars!'

Then a friendly young man joined them.
'Good evening, ladies. My name is Tootan. I have a special permit to show you the turtles.'

Lizzie screamed excitedly, 'Turtles! Turtles! I love turtles! Can we, Mom? Please?'

Mrs Steele smiled. This was part of the birthday adventure.

'Ssh, little girl,' Tootan said. 'We must be so still and quiet that we blend in with the night.'

The girls pretended they were little birds and they tiptoed lightly across the sand. They followed the beam of Tootan's torch.

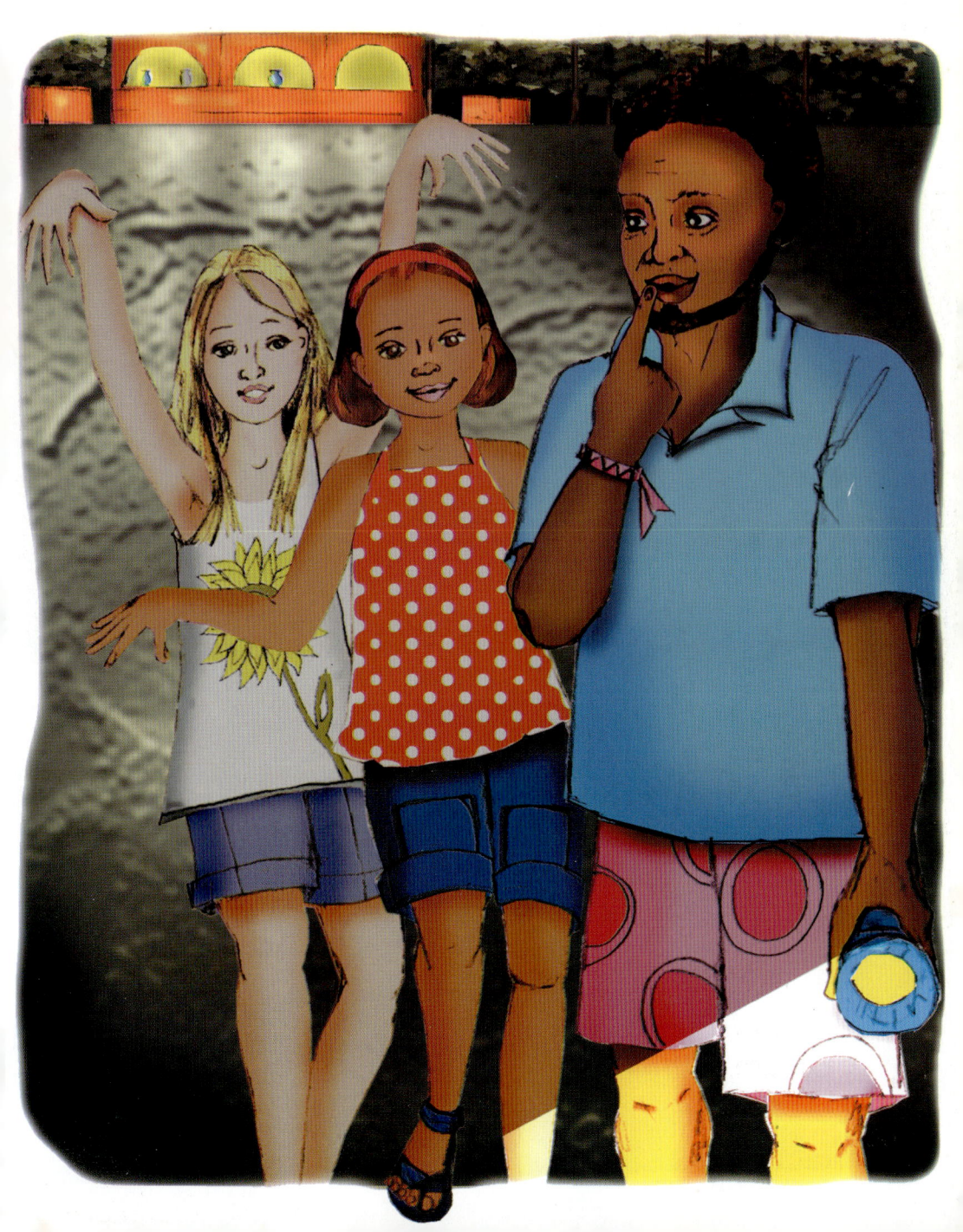

Tootan flashed the light and they hurried to him. He stretched out his hand. In his palm was a tiny turtle.

'It's so teeny-weeny,' whispered Alex and the girls giggled as they touched it gently.

'This is only a baby hatchling,' he explained. 'It's probably the last one from the nest. It's making its way back to the sea. Turtles lay eggs here from March to August every year.'

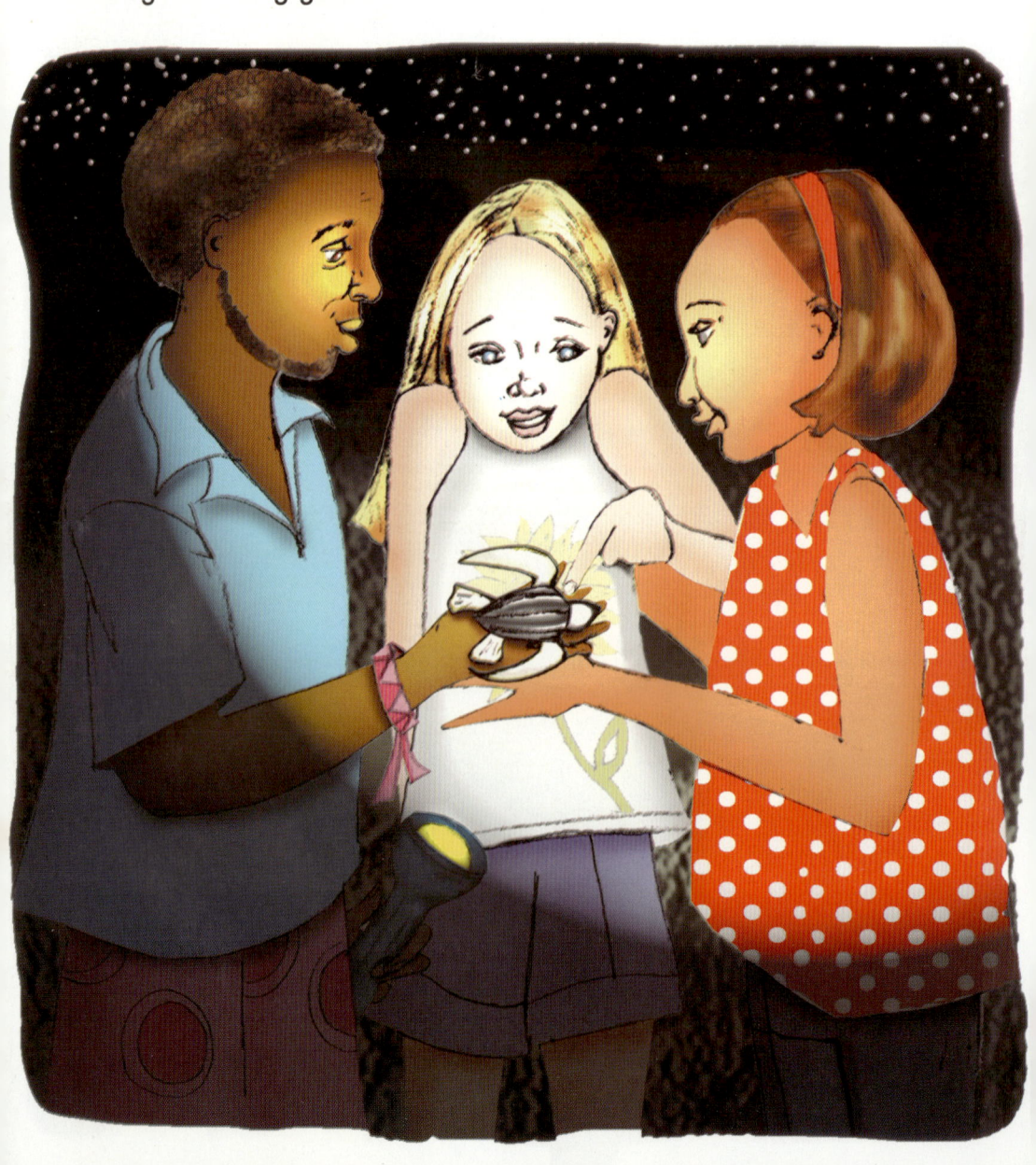

The girls, arm in arm, huddled close to Lizzy's mother. The lights of the guest house disappeared in the distance.

Tootan switched off his torch and they crept slowly up to a big, black rock. Without the light, they saw only shadows.

Lizzy was trembling with the mystery and excitement. They could hear movement in the sand. Tootan wrapped the torch around his T-shirt and flicked it back on.

'It's not a rock at all!' whispered Lizzy. 'It's a giant turtle!'

'It's the best I've seen,' whispered Alex.

'This is a giant leather back turtle. She's laying eggs. It's very safe, she won't harm you,' said Tootan.

He let the girls touch the turtle as he spoke. 'Her back isn't made of shell,' he said. 'It's layers of tough skin. It feels smooth and hard, doesn't it?'
'Like leather,' said Lizzy.

'Her head is cool and rough,' whispered Alex. 'And sandy too! And look! Her flippers are as long as Lizzy's legs.'

Lizzy stretched out a leg. 'Not quite as long,' she protested.

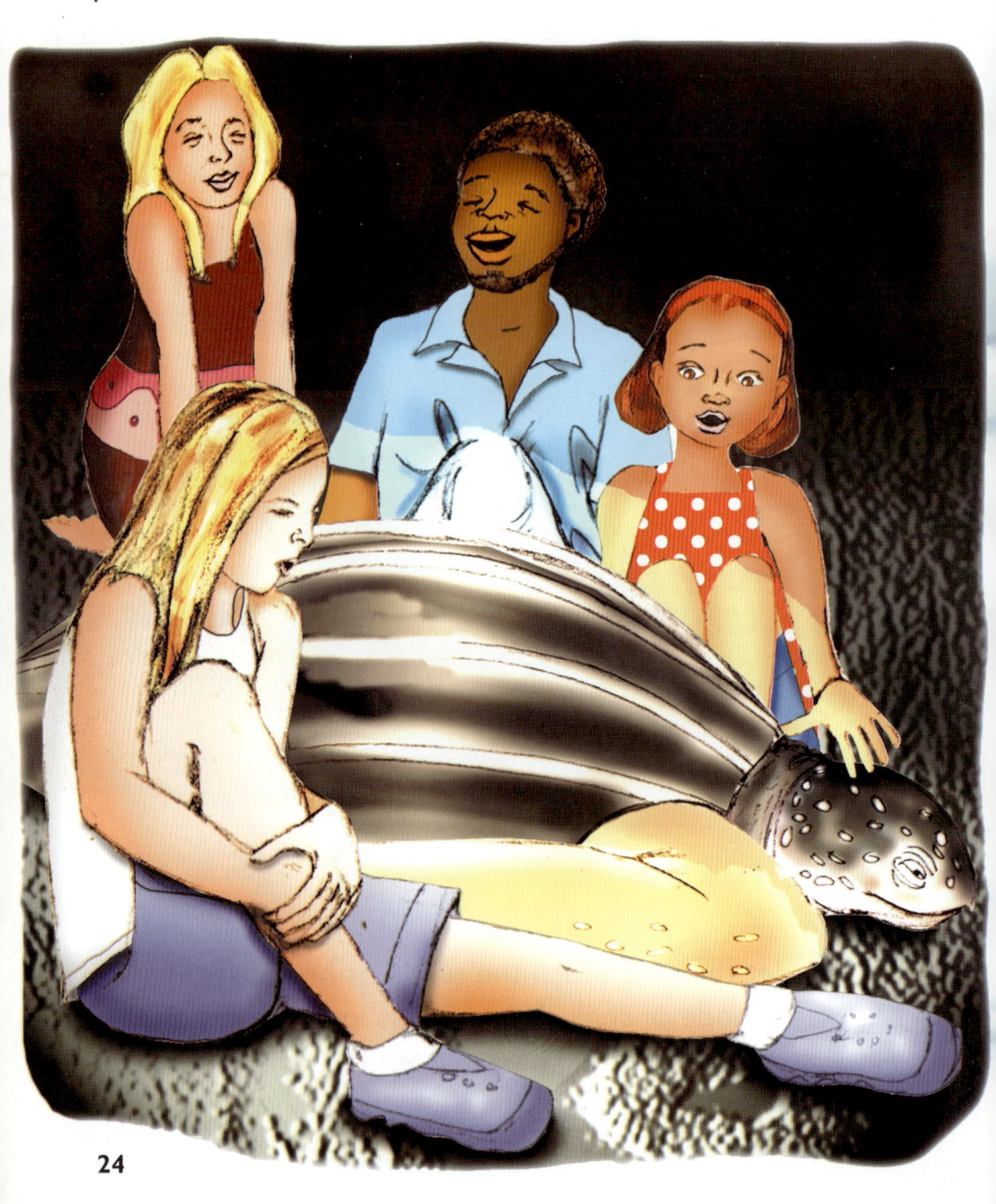

Lizzy lay in the sand, almost rubbing noses with the turtle. 'Tootan, is she crying?'

Tootan explained, 'Those tears protect her eyes from the sand. She isn't sad or hurt. Don't you worry, Lizzy. I'm a ranger and I protect the leather backs and teach people about them. That's my job.'

It was hard to keep count of the eggs as the mother turtle laid them. They fell deep into the sandy nest.

'About eighty or ninety,' said Tootan. He took one out gently and they felt it.

'Its shell's like white jelly,' said Lizzy. 'It's not hard like chicken eggs.'

'And this will become a hatchling,' said Alex. 'Then it will grow up to be a big, big turtle like this one.'

The next morning, Lizzy's night time adventure seemed like a dream. Sitting on the beach after breakfast, she pointed out the soft, white broken eggshells of the hatchlings to Alex and her mother.

'So it was real!' she whispered.

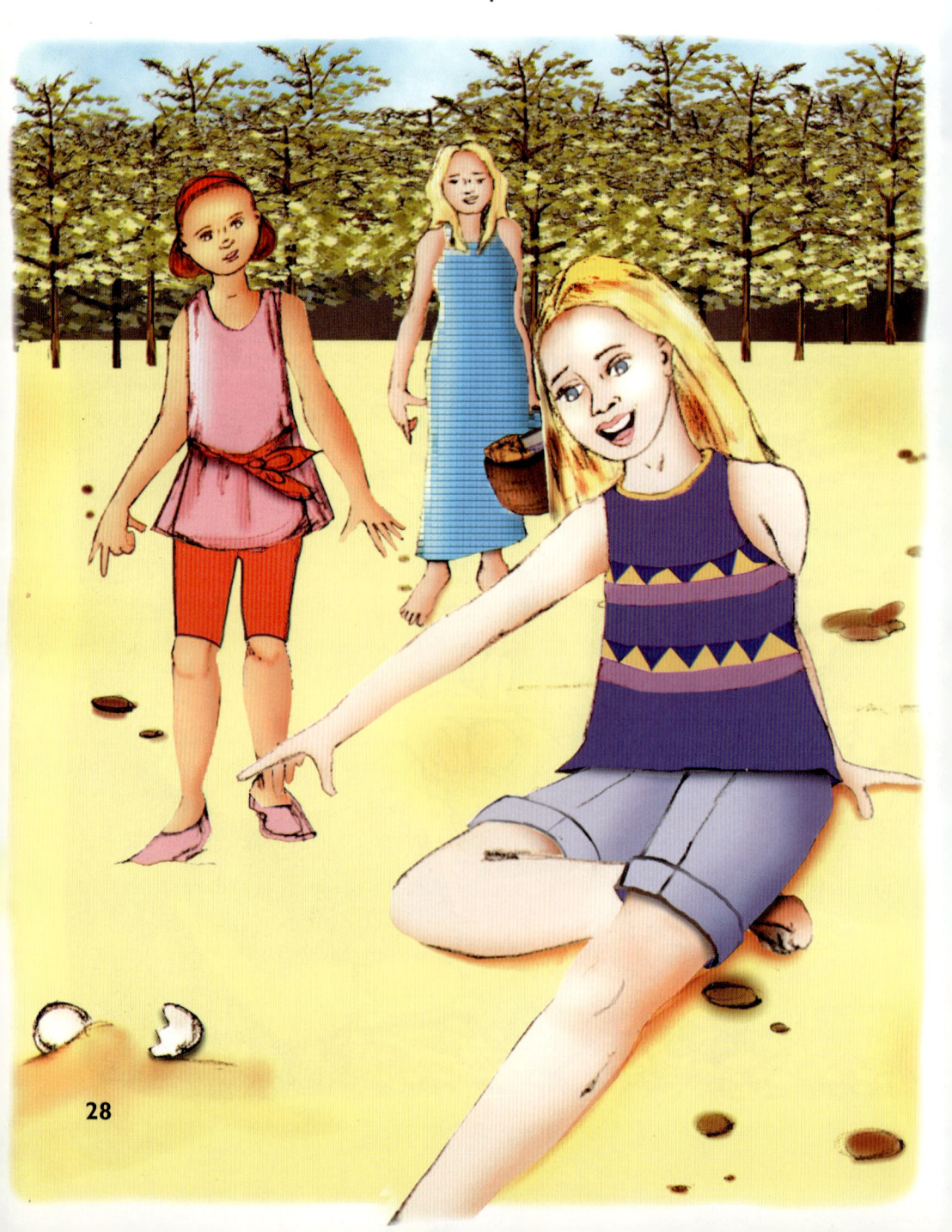

As Lizzy looked out to sea, the waves seemed to call her in for a game.
'The crests of the waves are like fingers,' she said. 'Look! They're tickling the water's back.'

'The car's all packed, girls. Ready to go?' called her mother.

Lizzy turned round. 'Hey, Mom, the waves are inviting us in. One last swim … pleeeease.'

Her mother nodded and the two friends took off their shorts and tops. Lizzy danced and hopped across the sharp stones and splashed into the sea without much fuss.

'Mom, you're right!' she called out. 'It's great to belong to two places. I belong to Scotland and to Trinidad as well! I'm a Scottish-Island girl!'

In My Father's Village Michael Palmer 0-333-56866-4
Striped Paint Rosina Umelo 0-333-56865-6
The Slow Chameleon and Shammy's Bride David Cobb 0-333-57728-0
The Walking Talking Flying ABC David Cobb 0-333-56864-8
Raindrops In Africa Margaret House 0-333-58723-5
Sing It, Do It David Cobb 0-333-58721-9
No Problem! Rosina Umelo 0-333-58722-7
Ten Ripe Mangoes David Cobb 0-333-60650-7
The Best Bed in The World Charlotte Mbali 0-333-61584-0
Under The Cotton Tree David Cobb 0-333-61828-9
Lucky Day! Lynn Kramer 0-333-68918-6
The Wake-up Whistler Marianna Brandt 0-333-72414-3
Ask Pungu-Pungu Rita Wooding 0-333-72636-7
Ping Pong P-Pan Barbara Applin 0-333-74142-0
Cabbages and Donkeys Margaret House 0-333-79168-1
The Wait and See Car Marianna Brandt 0-333-79169-X
Click! Flash! Barbara Applin 0-333-92077-5

Choose Me! Lynn Kramer 0-333-56867-2
Nondo The Cow Diane Rasteiro 0-333-57655-1
Sika In The Snow David Cobb 0-333-57672-1
Henry The Last Michael Palmer 0-333-58724-3
My Life On The Wing David Cobb 0-333-58725-1
The Radio Thief Anthony K Johnson 0-333-59514-9
The Grasshopper War Thokozile Chaane 0-333-61411-9
The Numberheads Robyn Roberts 0-333-61412-7
The All-Day Dreamer Karen W Mbugua and Geoff Baier 0-333-61651-0
Honeybrown And The Bees Jill Inyundo 0-333-64191-4
Lissa's Rainbow Dress Joyce Ama Addo 0-333-63310-5
The Bug Collector Gillian Leggat 0-333-63309-1
A Job On The Moon Michael Montgomery 0-333-64330-5
The Lily Pool Jill Inyundo 0-333-67083-3
Want To Be A Strongman? Michael Montgomery 0-333-69877-0
The Cowrie Seekers Shelley Davidow 0-333-68833-3
Ibuka And The Lost Children Sibylla Martin 0-333-68834-1
The Angry Mountain Claudette Megan Adams 0-333-74144-7
A Goat Called Gloria Nola Turkington 0-333-79171-1
The Boy Who Made Cars Stephen Alumenda 0-333-79170-3
The Big Bad Snake Kweku Duodu Asumang 0-333-79809-0
The Scottish-Island Girl Joanne Gail Johnson 0-333-92991-0

Chichi And The Termites Wendy Ijioma 0-333-57696-9
The Boy Who Ate A Hyena James G D Ngumy 0-333-57694-2
Tickets For The Zed Band Lynn Kramer 0-333-57695-0
Knife Boy Michael Montgomery 0-333-59513-0
Chichi's Nature Diary Wendy Ijioma 0-333-59512-2
Fair Shares Lynn Kramer 0-333-59511-4
Paa Bena And The New Canoe Phyllis Addy 0-333-59857-1
Chimpanzee Rescue Margaret House 0-333-60651-5
The Calabash And The Box Bobson Sesay 0-333-61826-2
Check, Come Here! Edison Yongai 0-333-61827-0
You Can't Grow Footballs From Seeds Margaret Spencer 0-333-62218-9
Pepi Mazamban, Mender of Cars, Age 10 James Mason 0-333-63308-3
Water Girl Michael Montgomery 0-333-64329-1
Two Eggs For The President Marianna Brandt 0-333-66810-3
Search For The Stone Bird Shelley Davidow 0-333-69876-2
Tofu in Trouble Dawn Ridgway 0-333-68200-9
Fisherwoman Effie Adrienne 0-333-74143-9
The Taming of Pudding Pan Berna McIntosh 0-333-74141-2
The Clay Animals Gabriel Ellison 0-333-79808-2

POETRY
On The Poetry Bus ed. David Cobb 0-333-64070-5
Sometimes When It Rains Achirri Chi-Bikom 0-333-63307-5
Riding A Rainbow Achirri Chi-Bikom 0-333-67160-0